## About the Book

One couldn't help but admire young Theodore Roosevelt. He suffered from asthma—a disease which made it difficult to breathe. But Theodore loved to play and explore nature and was determined to grow strong!

Theodore's determination and enthusiasm led him to a colorful life . . . as a cowboy, soldier, adventurer, and politician.

Sibyl Hancock and Joseph Ciardiello have created a fascinating biography of the man who became the twenty-sixth president of the United States.

Theodore Roosevelt

A See and Read Biography

# THEODORE ROOSEVELT

## BY SIBYL HANCOCK

ILLUSTRATED BY
## JOSEPH CIARDIELLO

G. P. Putnam's Sons          New York

Text copyright © 1978 by Sibyl Hancock
Illustrations copyright © 1978 by Joseph Ciardiello
All rights reserved. Published simultaneously in
Canada by Longman, Canada Limited, Toronto.
Printed in the United States of America
06209
Library of Congress Cataloging in Publication Data
Hancock, Sibyl. Theodore Roosevelt. (A See and Read Biography)
SUMMARY: An easy-to-read biography of the twenty-sixth
President of the United States.
1. Roosevelt, Theodore, Pres. U. S., 1858-1919—
Juvenile literature. 2. Presidents—United States—
Biography—Juvenile Literature. [1. Roosevelt, Theodore,
Pres. U. S., 1858-1919. 2. Presidents]
I. Ciardiello, Joseph. II. Title
E757.H24     1977     973.91 1'0924     (B)     (92)     77-22614
ISBN 0-399-61107-X lib. bdg.

For Agnes Hamm and Ruth Morton,
two remarkable English teachers

Young Theodore Roosevelt often woke in the middle of the night. He would sit up in bed and gasp for air. He had an illness called asthma. The asthma made him weak and made it difficult for him to breathe.

Some winter nights, Theodore's father took him out in the carriage. The boy would shiver as they drove through the dark streets. But the cold night air helped him breathe easier. His father told him to be brave. He said one day Theodore would get better.

Theodore Roosevelt was born in New York City on October 27, 1858. He was the second oldest child in the family. He had one brother and two sisters.

They were a happy family. They had picnics, and swam and went

on hikes together. Theodore tried
his best to keep up with his
brother and sisters, but often he
could only watch them play.

Theodore wanted so much to
run about with them. But most of
the time he was too tired to play

for long. He made up his mind that someday he would be strong enough to play as long and as hard as he liked. He would be strong enough to do anything he wanted.

Sometimes Theodore would lie on the ground and watch ants busy at work. He thought how wonderful it was that even the tiny ants were strong. Theodore liked to catch butterflies, bees, spiders, and beetles. He learned how to mount them. Sometimes, when he had to stay indoors, he would study his collection of insects and spiders. Then he would close his eyes and pretend he was outside, running in the sun with the bees and butterflies.

Sometimes Theodore's interest in animals and insects got him into trouble. Maids were scared of the mice he had in a cage and the snakes in jars. Once, the woman who did the laundry found Theodore's turtles in the washtubs. She left and did not come back. Another time, Theodore found a dead mouse. He wanted to study it before burying it. So he put the mouse in the icebox until he had more time to look at it. His mother was not pleased.

Theodore wasn't well enough to go to school. He took lessons from a teacher who lived nearby. He

longed to be with his friends. He missed sitting in class with them. What fun it would be to share jokes and laugh together.

When he was alone, Theodore enjoyed reading. He liked to read about sailors and pirates. He could forget about being sick and dream of brave adventures on the high seas. His books took him to far-away places.

Theodore read a lot about cowboys. He wished he had a horse.
And when he was nine years old,
his father gave him a Shetland
pony. It was like a dream come
true. Whenever he was well
enough, Theodore took his pony

for long rides. Someday, maybe, he would have a chance to go west and be a cowboy. He was determined to grow strong. He would not let asthma get the best of him!

Theodore wasn't sick all of the time. One day, when he felt well, he went with some friends to practice shooting at targets. Time and again his friends shot at targets he couldn't see. Theodore wondered if there might be something wrong with his eyes.

Theodore's father took him to a doctor. The doctor said Theodore could not see far-off things and told him he needed glasses. When he got them, Theodore was surprised by how beautiful everything looked. He could see trees and clouds clearly for the first time.

When Theodore was thirteen, he wanted to go to a summer camp. He was tired of staying at

home when everyone else was going on trips and having fun. When he got to camp, Theodore did not enjoy it much. There were two boys who always teased him and made fun of him because he was small and slow at games. Theodore tried to fight them, but he never won.

Theodore was angry with himself for being too weak to fight back and win. He told his father that he wanted to work at building his muscles. So his father built a gymnasium on the third floor of their home with swings and seesaws and a punching bag. There were weights to lift and bars to climb over.

Theodore worked in the gym
every day. He would exercise for
hours on end. Sometimes Theodore's friends came to play in the
gym. They liked to swing on the
bars and hit the punching bag.

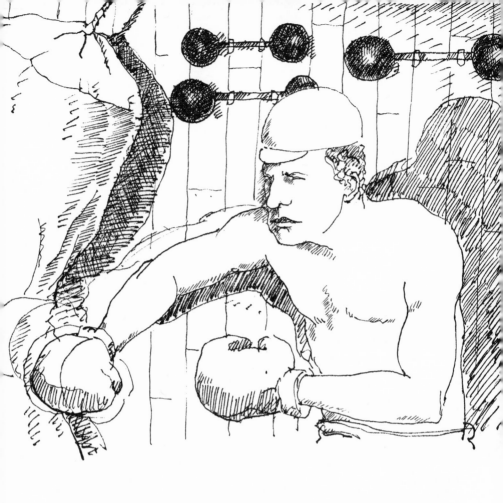

But Theodore was not playing.
Day after day he worked on the
bars and lifted weights. Slowly he
began to grow stronger and taller.
In time, Theodore became a
healthy young man.

Now that he was feeling well, Theodore began to study more seriously. But he had to work hard to make up for all the school he had missed.

Theodore learned fast. Soon he was ready to go to college. He was accepted at Harvard University in Cambridge, Massachusetts. He found that he was interested in everything. He studied hard and made good grades. He was fun, and everyone liked him immediately.

Theodore had always thought he would become a scientist. But at college he decided to study his-

tory and law instead. He was particularly interested in politics. He learned everything he could about how the government worked.

Not long after he finished college, Theodore married a pretty girl named Alice Lee. After a honeymoon in Europe, Theodore and Alice came home to live in New York City.

Theodore was still interested in government. He wanted to go into politics. People told him that politics was rough and unfair. They said there were many dishonest men controlling government. But Theodore wanted to prove that honest men could run for office and win.

Theodore wanted to become a New York State senator. Not many people had ever heard of him, so he began to make speeches throughout the state. He told people how he would fight for honest government if he were elected. People liked what he had to say.

Theodore Roosevelt won the election. He worked hard as a state senator, trying to make good laws.

One day at work, Theodore was handed a message. It said that his wife had just given birth to a baby daughter. Theodore hurried home. He wanted to see Alice and their new baby.

Theodore's young wife was very weak, and the next day she died. A few hours later, on the very same day, his mother died of typhoid fever. Theodore was overcome with sadness. He tried to go back to work in politics, but his heart was not in it.

Theodore had always wanted to go west. He decided that now might be the time to give it a try. He left his tiny daughter with his sister and went to North Dakota, where he bought a ranch.

At first the cowboys teased him because he wore glasses and fancy clothes. But they soon learned that Theodore wanted to work hard. Before long he was as good a cowboy as any of them.

One time, he was herding cattle, and they became frightened and stampeded. Runaway cattle are dangerous, but Theodore was an excellent rider, and he was determined to save the herd. He rode for nearly two days without rest, and he didn't go home until the last of the cattle had been rounded up.

One winter, Theodore was made a deputy sheriff so he could help catch some thieves who had stolen a boat for their getaway. Theodore and two of his men followed them in another boat. They traveled miles before they captured the thieves at gunpoint. When they tried to head back down the river to the nearest jail, ice blocked their way.

Theodore left his men with the boat and struck out on land, alone with the two outlaws. The weather was bitter cold. Day after day he marched the thieves over icy

ground. At night, he made them take off their shoes so they could not get away. When they finally reached the jail, Theodore had walked forty cold miles and had lost many hours of sleep.

Theodore spent two years on the ranch before he felt ready to return to New York and to politics. Soon after coming home, he met Edith Carrow. She had been a childhood friend. Theodore and Edith were married. They took his little daughter with them when they moved into a pretty house on Long Island called Sagamore Hill. Eventually, they had five more children.

Theodore was a good father. He always found time for his children. He had not forgotten how he longed to play as a child. He played with his children so much that his wife said he was like a boy himself.

In 1898, Theodore Roosevelt was busy serving the government as assistant secretary of the Navy. That year, the United States went to war against Spain. The United States wanted to help free Cuba, an island country near Florida, from Spanish rule.

Theodore Roosevelt joined the Army. He was given the rank of colonel. He led a group of men known as the Rough Riders. Many of Theodore's cowboy friends joined the Army to fight beside him.

In Cuba the weather was extremely hot. When Roosevelt's

men tried to sleep, they found lizards and mosquitoes all around them. Many of the men became sick with fever. Theodore visited them every day.

Roosevelt helped win one of the most important battles in Cuba. He led the charge on San Juan Hill. Roosevelt was the first man to reach the top of the hill. Many Rough Riders were shot, but Theodore's courage helped his men win the battle.

The United States soon won the war. When Theodore Roosevelt returned home, he was honored as a hero. Crowds of people cheered him.

Roosevelt was elected governor of New York not long after the war ended. While he held office, he proved to many people that he believed in an honest government. He fought dishonesty in big business. Many giant corporations had paid politicians to pass laws that helped big business but hurt ordinary people. Roosevelt tried to stop this from happening.

A short time later, President William McKinley picked Theodore Roosevelt as his choice for vice-president. The two men won the election in 1900.

Theodore Roosevelt had been

vice-president for only six months
when President McKinley was
shot. If the president died, Theodore would become the new president.

After a while it seemed that President McKinley was going to get well. Roosevelt took his wife and children on a trip. They were climbing a mountain when Roosevelt got word that President McKinley was dying.

Roosevelt wanted to see the president before he died. Quickly he packed his clothes. He jumped into a wagon that he had hired.

He shouted for the driver to hurry. It was foggy and dark. But Roosevelt was determined to get to the railroad station.

The road was muddy. The horses raced and slipped over the

mountain path. It was a dangerous
ride, but he would not turn back.

When Roosevelt reached the station, he learned that President McKinley was dead. Theodore Roosevelt became the twenty-sixth president of the United States. At forty-two years of age, he was the youngest man to reach the country's highest office.

Roosevelt was president for the next seven years. The American people loved him. They liked to call him T. R. or Teddy.

Theodore was a busy president. He never seemed to get tired of working. The door to his office was open to anyone who wanted to see him.

Sometimes old Rough Riders or cowboys visited him. And he happily talked over old times with them.

The White House was as noisy and as full of fun as any home in the country. Children ran through the halls shouting and laughing. Sometimes Roosevelt joined in big pillow fights with them.

There were times when important visitors tripped over toy wagons left in doorways.

Once, Roosevelt's sons even brought a pet pony into the White House. What confusion that caused!

Theodore Roosevelt tried to make life better for the American people. Many of his actions helped people all over the world.

While he was the president, the Panama Canal was built. Ships no longer had to go all the way around South America to get from the Atlantic Ocean to the Pacific Ocean.

Roosevelt received much praise when he helped make peace between Russia and Japan. The countries had been at war. The president held many meetings with men from the two countries. He listened to their arguments. He tried to be patient with them, which was difficult for him. He had always been impatient. But peace was made between Japan and Russia. Roosevelt received the Nobel Peace Prize for his part in ending the war.

One of the most important things he did was to make people think about conservation. He was concerned about wildlife. He enjoyed hunting, but he believed it was important to keep hunters from killing too many of our birds and animals. Until this time, few people had thought about wildlife becoming extinct. Theodore wanted to make certain that birds and animals would be plentiful for sportsmen and nature lovers of future generations.

Roosevelt used his power as president to set aside land to make many national forests. He believed that when trees were cut down, more trees should be planted in their place. He also wanted to protect forests from the terrible fires that often destroyed them. So he set up the first forest-ranger stations. Over the years

forest rangers have saved many
trees by spotting forest fires just as
they begin.

Roosevelt also made plans to
bring water to the dry areas in the
West. Great dams that formed
large lakes were built on western
rivers. The water from these lakes
was used to irrigate dry land. More
than three million acres that had

been too dry to be used as farm-
land could now grow crops.

When Theodore was president,
five new national parks were
created. He also passed a law to
protect historic spots and natural
wonders like the Petrified Forest
in Arizona. These places would
also be national parks that people
could visit and enjoy.

When Roosevelt's years in the White House were over, he and his family moved back to Sagamore Hill. Roosevelt had no plans for relaxing in the country. He loved excitement and travel. So he took one of his sons with him to visit Africa.

One day, when they were far into the jungle, a rhinoceros charged out of the trees. It ran straight for Roosevelt. There was no time for making a mistake. Roosevelt took careful aim with his gun and shot. The rhinoceros

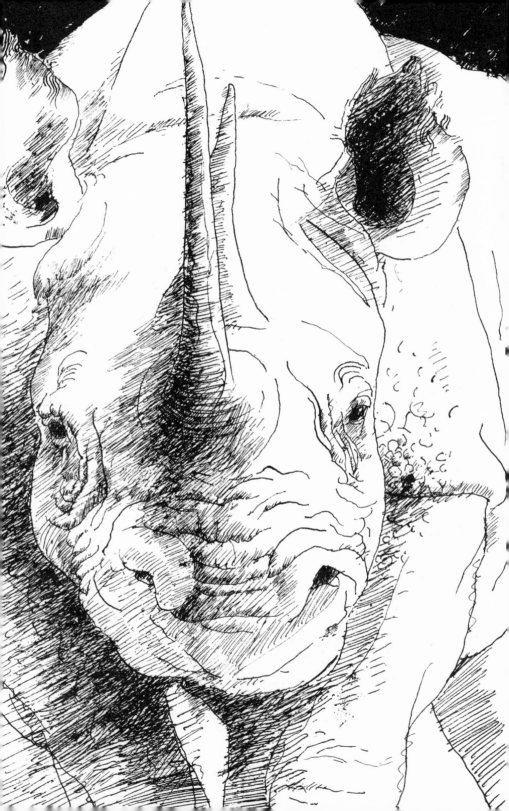

dropped dead only thirteen steps away from him. It had been a close brush with death.

Roosevelt took two of his sons with him on another trip, this time to South America. He wanted to explore the jungles. The trip was dangerous. People asked him not to go.

But Roosevelt would not change his mind. "It is my last chance to be a boy again," he said, smiling.

In the great jungles, the men saw mosquitoes and fire ants and red wasps. There were huge snakes everywhere.

They traveled down a river that was one thousand miles long. It was known as the River of Doubt.

No white person had ever before
explored its full length. Roosevelt
drew a map to show the river's
course, and later the river was
named after Roosevelt.

Before the trip was over, Roosevelt became sick with jungle fever. For the rest of his life, he never felt really well again.

Theodore Roosevelt died at Sagamore Hill when he was sixty years old. People all over the world mourned his death.

All his life, Theodore Roosevelt had been a fighter. He fought sickness as a boy, and he grew strong. When he was older, he fought for freedom and for honesty in American government. And for this he will be remembered as one of our greatest presidents.

## About the Author

SIBYL HANCOCK has written several children's books, including *Mario's Mystery Machine* and *The Blazing Hills*, for Putnam's. She lives in Houston, Texas, where she received her Bachelor of Arts degree from the University of Houston. Besides being a juvenile book critic for the Houston *Chronicle* and a member of several writers' groups, Ms. Hancock is an amateur astronomer and enjoys collecting old children's books.

## About the Artist

JOSPEH CIARDIELLO is a graduate of Parsons School of Design and has a Bachelor of Fine Arts degree. His illustrations have appeared in numerous national publications and in several Society of Illustrators Annual Exhibits. Mr. Ciardiello also illustrated the Putnam books *Buffalo Bill* and *The Great Houdini*. He lives on Staten Island, New York.